Little Pebble

Celebrate

Autumn Leaves

by Erika L. Shores

raintree
a Capstone company — publishers for children

Raintree is an imprint of Capstone Global Library Limited, a company incorporated in England and Wales having its registered office at 7 Pilgrim Street, London, EC4V 6LB – Registered company number: 6695582

www.raintree.co.uk
myorders@raintree.co.uk

Editorial Credits
Edited by Mari Bolte and Erika Shores, designed by Cynthia Della-Rovere, picture research by Svetlana Zhurkin production by Morgan Walters

ISBN 978 1 4747 0297 3 (hardback)
19 18 17 16 15
10 9 8 7 6 5 4 3 2 1

ISBN 978 1 4747 0302 4 (paperback)
20 19 18 17 16 15
10 9 8 7 6 5 4 3 2 1

British Library Cataloguing in Publication Data
A full catalogue record for this book is available from the British Lib

Photo Credits
Dreamstime: Robin Van Olderen, 12, SandraRBarba, 6—7, Smellme, 26—27; Shutterstock: Aaron Amat, 27 (top), ala737, 13 (bottom), Al bjogroet, 11 (top), Black Sheep Media (grass), throughout, Chantal d throughout, creative, 10, e2dan, 13 (top), Eric Isselee, cover, back cov Gerrit_de_Vries, 14 (top), 17, Jez Bennett, 14 (bottom), John Michael Evan Potter, 9, Maggy Meyer, 28—29, MattiaATH, 8, Mogens Trolle, 15 (bottom), moizhusein, 20—21, 23, Moments by Mullineux, 5, Sean Stanton, 19, Serge Vero, 24, Stuart G. Porter, 22

Printed and Bound in China.

Contents

Colourful trees

Red, yellow and orange
cover the forest.

Autumn is here.

Leaves can change colour in autumn. Oak leaves change to red and brown.

7

Maple leaves turn red, orange and yellow.

9

Round aspen leaves
turn gold.

Evergreen trees
do not change colour.
Their needles stay green.

Falling leaves

Autumn leaves die.
They fall to
the ground.

Listen! Leaves crunch
as you walk.

16

Rake leaves into piles.

Then jump in!

The trees are empty.

They wait for spring.

Glossary

forest large area thickly covered with trees and plants; forests are also called woodlands

gold yellow-brown colour

needle sharp, green leaf on an evergreen tree

rake gather or move using a tool with a long handle

spring season after winter and before summer

Read more

All About Leaves (All About Plants), Claire Throp (Raintree, 2014)

What Can You See in Autumn? (Seasons), Sian Smith (Raintree, 2014)

Websites

www.bbc.co.uk/gardening/digin/your_space/patch.shtml
Celebrate autumn by growing and harvesting fruit and vegetables in your garden or on your windowsill. Follow the BBC's step-by-step picture guide to help you get started.

www.naturedetectives.org.uk/autumn/
Download wildlife ID sheets, pick up some great autumn crafting ideas and collect recipes for some delicious autumn cooking projects on this website.

Index